One Night in the City

Liverpool

Wednesday 25th May 2005

by Ian Leech

First Published 2005 by Countyvise Limited,
14 Appin Road, Birkenhead, Wirral CH41 9HH

British Library Cataloguing in Publication Data.
A catalogue record for this book is available from the British Library.

ISBN 1 901231 55 0

A Night in the City

"Look, if you want to go home at half-time and listen to the second half on the radio, you only have to say".

That was the sympathetic offering made to my daughter at about twenty five past eight on Wednesday 25 May. Sat on a bar stool, head resting on the palm of her hand, tears in her eyes, it seemed a trivial gesture, but it needed saying, if anything to save her from further torture.

You see, whilst my beloved daughter is a red through and through, my allegiance is toward the blue of Merseyside. My support of The Toffees goes back to the days of Harvey, Kendal and Ball with Big Joe Royle leading the line, whilst Melissa is a devotee of the reds due in no small part to Michael Owen.

She'd been waiting for this moment for over a month. Ever since Garcia's goal that shouldn't have been, but was, allowed Liverpool the chance to go for a fifth European Champions League title, Mel had been on a high. As the final grew ever closer she got higher and higher, especially as following the victory over Chelsea I'd promised to take her to watch the final in a bar in the centre of Liverpool. Like all fathers I am prone to the odd lapse in concentration and I must have had one the moment I agreed to her suggestion of travelling to the city.

So at about 12.15pm on Wednesday 25 May, we set off from the Midlands up the M6 to Liverpool....

3.03pm
Parking up at Albert Dock, we get the first signs that something major is happening in the city.

Two old boys discuss the forthcoming game, but little do they or Milan know that the cup is already in Liverpool and is going nowhere.

3.05pm
Time for a family album shot of Mel by the River Mersey. This is being done to appease her mother, but also to take her mind off forthcoming events. Nerves are beginning to take a hold and the toilet had already been visited twice!

.49pm

fter strolling around the
lbert Dock, we visit one
r two shops, and then
ead for the city centre.
ports shops are doing a
paring trade on "Gerrard
" shirts, whilst in the
entre itself, more and
nore replica kits begin to
urface. Even at this hour
nough with just under
ur hours to the big kick
ff… finger nails are
king a hammering!

3.51pm

Mel cannot walk past a souvenir stand without wanting to check it thoroughly, so consequently we're having to visit each and every one.

I get the impression the owner of this place made a late decision to tap into the European market as there seems to be a fair few non-Liverpool items in amongst the flags, badges and scarves. Speaking of tapping, a Chelsea scarf has also found its way in amongst the stock…. Whatever happened to them?

This is the first of many banners we see as we stroll around the town. It's always nice to see grammatically correct works of art too! Apostrophes in the right place! It's still relatively quiet at the moment and we're trying to sort out our bearings, making sure we know our way back to the car should the need arise!

4.05pm
More supporters take to the streets and these lads have gone as far as getting matching hats for the occasion. One supporter is practising his goal celebrations whilst behind him life in the city goes on as normal. Mel has bought two badges from a street seller that she has pinned to her baseball cap. I tried to persuade her to buy a blue one, but she wouldn't have it!

.07pm

defining moment. As e walk through the city, a uy with an air horn blasts ut "Da, da, da da da… nd from nowhere upporters and shoppers like respond with a pontaneous chant of LIVERPOOL". It's like a ake up call and all of a udden there is a real buzz round the place. Such is he atmosphere and pontaneity of the noment that the guy arrying the child goes hands free."

.14pm

As the centre of the city begins to turn red, we decide it's time to find somewhere to watch the game and we head for Concert quare. Already, with three and half hours still to go to kick off, the Square is alive with supporters getting in the party mood.

4.15pm

The pints are lined up, the special offers are being advertised and the silly hats are in place. It can only be a cup final!

4.16pm

I pick out these three guys modelling the latest in footballing attire. From the eighties replica on the right and seventies shirt in the centre, to the "mine's in the wash, so I'll wear my scarf round my belt" look of the present day.

4.24pm
Still in Concert Square and minute by minute more and more Liverpool fans are arriving. These supporters gather outside the Walkabout bar. The atmosphere is building by the second as the excitement grows.

4.26pm
In Walkabout we meet these two Irish guys. Both admit they are a "wee bit tipsy" and we also learn they have travelled over from Ireland, forgotten their credit cards, were in a hotel but weren't sure where and didn't really care where they slept. If Liverpool win they reckon they won't need a hotel anyway as they'll sleep wherever they happen to fall over!

4.27pm
In Walkabout at half past four and Andy Gray hasn't even got his cardboard pitch and tiddlywinks out yet. Spaces are at a premium but it seems like a great place to watch the game. Flags hang from the balconies and walls and the atmosphere is electric as chants of "Steve Gerrard, Gerrard…" ring out.

4.27pm
Still in Walkabout, the bar staff are doing a sterling job serving alcohol to the masses. Fans are exchanging views and the possibility of Harry Kewell playing and what role he will occupy is debated, as is the possibility that when the cup is won there won't be enough alcohol in Liverpool to cope with demand!

4.33pm
A view from the balcony in Walkabout and still the bar staff keep going. There are a few spaces by the door, but it won't be long before they're taken.

4.33pm
More views across the balcony and "best positions" are being secured long before kick off. Above the sounds of constant chatter I hear for the first (and not the last) time those immortal words ..."I'm just off to the loo, save my place won't you?"

4.45pm
Three hours before kick off we decide to leave Walkabout and get a bite to eat and a breath of fresh air. Outside in Concert Square the number of fans has more than doubled with chants of "Oh when the reds… go marching in…" booming out across the Square.

4.47pm
Wouldn't fancy standing behind that guy in the pub, but he seems friendly enough and supporters queue up to have their pictures taken with him.

4.49pm

All roads lead to the pubs and the big screens. Back in the centre, fans head for their favourite bar in preparation for the game.

4.50pm

Boys and Girls come out to play and as they walk along pose for the camera. In the background a Police camera van is parked up for the evening, the screens inside are all turned on, but unluckily for the boys in blue, they can't be tuned into ITV or Sky Sports!

5.04pm

Back to Concert Square and groups of fans stand around discussing the night ahead. In amongst the sea of red one lady fan proudly wears her Liverpool away strip and once more chants and songs start to ring around the square.

5.04pm
"With hope in your heart, and you'll ne-ver walk alone, you'll ne-ver walk alone…"
Heard for the first (and not the last) time in Concert Square!

5.10pm
We've made our way back to Walkabout, but due to Mel being two months short of her 18th birthday we can't get back in. Undeterred we cross the square to the Klass bar as another chorus of "Oh when the reds, go marching in ……" fills the air!

5.32pm
Can't decide which flag to take with you to watch the game? This guy has the answer. Sew them all together to create the Ultimate Flag!

7.09pm

With limited staff and the insistence that the big screen can't be viewed til 7pm, we stand and queue for an hour and a half, reading the Liverpool Echo and talking to other fans… and then news filters through that Kewell is starting… opinion is divided!

7.09pm

The balcony at Klass is becoming increasingly crowded as excitement reaches fever pitch. As the players make their first appearances on the big screen, cheers ring out, along with songs about Rafael Benitez, Steven Gerrard and Scouser Tommy.

7.10pm

As more and more fans crowd onto the balcony, new songs spring up and to the tune of Forever in Blue Jeans by Neil Diamond comes… "….Money talks, but it don't sing and dance and it don't walk….their Mourinho wants our Stevie G, but he'd much rather be… winning the Champions League!"

7.14pm

With more and more supporters crowding onto the balcony and limited staff to supervise we decide to leave and try to find somewhere a little less crowded, but with only half an hour to kick off and a sea of red between us and the exit door, time is against us!

7.29pm

Fifteen minutes to kick off and we've found a pub in the centre of Liverpool called The Blob! A complete mix of young and old fans, the atmosphere is amazing! The adverts on ITV are ignored as last minute tactics and who's round it is, are discussed!

7.43pm

It's all about to kick off! The reds and the whites take to the pitch and a roar fills the pub… Mel takes off her hat and the game begins…then just after the game started… it all went quiet and then totally silent. Half time comes with Andy Gray declaring game over! Some fans sit in tears, quite a few leave and a distraught Mel puts her hat back on…and then came 8:58pm and suddenly things began to change…

8.58pm

At 8:58pm a little light appears at the end of the Mersey Tunnel, it's only a little light, but it's enough to get fans singing and smiling again! Gerrard pulls a goal back for the reds and in The Blob… celebrations are undertaken!

8.59pm

The celebrations have just about died down, most fans are glued to the screen in anticipation of a second goal… whilst others just need a stiff one… from the bar that is!

9.00pm

Vladimir Smicer sends Liverpool into raptures when his edge of the box strike beats the Milan keeper. Arms are held aloft, smiles get ever wider and another chorus of "Oh when the reds, go marching in, Oh when the reds go marching in, I wanna be in that number… Oh when the reds go marching in" shakes the walls of The Blob!

9.00pm

As the beer literally flows fans get showered. Mel is standing on a chair and is now convinced that the reason for the comeback is her hat and the two badges, bought before the game! Apparently, they have magic powers!

9.01pm

3-2 to Liverpool and the crowd are going wild! The light at the end of the Mersey Tunnel is now very bright! Could we be witnessing one of the greatest footballing comebacks of all time? This lady seems to think so!

9.03pm

Gerrard goes through, gets into the penalty area, he's brought down… PENALTY! The pub erupts and while in the background Milan players debate the decision on the TV, these two ladies pose for a picture…but will they be smiling in a minute or so?

9.04:32pm
One kick away from a magical comeback. Everyone needs to hold their nerve... Alonso steps up, the pressure is on, and The Blob falls silent for a brief moment! He takes his kick and the expression on the girl's faces tells the story... he's missed...

9.04:38pm
The city shakes as Alonso recovers to smash in the rebound after his penalty is saved. Fans jump on tables, dance in the streets, hug complete strangers and cry tears of joy as the Reds complete their amazing recovery!

From total despair to untold joy in six amazing minutes... and there's still half an hour of normal time to go!

9.05pm

As the game restarts, the fans celebrate. Hands are held in the air and not a drop of beer or lager is spilt. Perfect hand-eye co-ordination.

As the newspapers of the world start re-writing their back pages, the name of Rafael Benitez is chorused around The Blob time and time again. Still twenty five minutes to go, but surely it can't go wrong now... can it?

9.05pm

"They'll never believe me, but I'm going to text them the score anyway" Now where's that three button!

9.13pm
The TV at the top of this picture had the Racing Channel on earlier in the evening, which wasn't a bad thing during the first half… but now it's redundant and all eyes are fixated on the other two screens… and the remaining fifteen minutes!!

9.14pm
Mel joins in another chorus of You'll never walk alone… note that the hat is on and the magic badges are in place. It's at this point I wonder what she'd have done to me if she'd taken up my offer of going home at half time… best not think about it!

9.15pm

More new faces appear in the Blob and word spreads on the street of what is unfolding. My thoughts turn to a guy stood behind me during the first half who walked out after 45 minutes. As he left I didn't know whether to place my arm around him and console him or put in a call to the Samaritans on his behalf! I bet he's feeling better now!

9.19pm

The room is divided between the singers and the watchers. Some prefer to sing out loud and raise the roof, whilst others need to watch the game and concentrate on what's happening on screen... as full time edges nearer the tension is mounting once more... as if it ever went away!

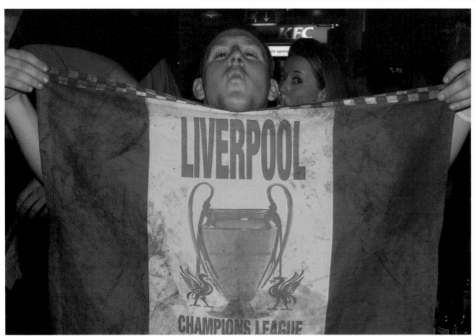

9.40pm
The end of normal time and it's 3-3. Extra time is about to start and this guy stops to pose for a picture. Will he wash the flag ever again or will superstition win the day?

9.59pm
Extra time in progress and all eyes turn back to the TV.

10.00pm
Extra time and the nails take another battering… how will they cope if it goes to penalties?

10.20pm
As extra time draws to a close this young lady holds her scarf aloft, whilst in the bottom left corner of the picture a couple have a kiss for good luck!

10.21pm

He's been stood on that table for ages… it would be bad luck to get down now!

10.21pm

Extra time is over…it's finished 3-3 and the European Champions League Final will be decided on penalties. As decisions are made as to who will take them, the fans gathered in The Blob are paying homage to their heroes, singing their names! Mel decides that she will watch the penalty shoot out and not turn away from the screen… that's a first!

10.22pm

Cometh the hour… cometh the man (or rather men)… and now is that hour! This supporter rallies the crowd for the final push! First up for taking a penalty is Milan's Serginho…

10.22pm

ITV announce that "the ITN Main News will follow this programme", Serginho misses the first penalty and yet again the pub goes wild… step up Didi Hamann for Liverpool.

10.24pm
Haman scores for Liverpool…
1-0 to the reds! The noise levels
increase yet further still!

10.24pm
The cheering just goes on and
on, those afraid to watch the
kicks can only guess at the score
by the volume or lack of
cheering from inside the bars!

10.25pm
The penalties continue to go Liverpool's way with only Riise having his kick saved… Smicer buries his kick and the fans know they're almost there.

10.28:58pm
All eyes on the TV screen and this captures the moment when Dudek saves Shevchenko's kick and Liverpool win the European Champions League for the 5th time.

Ten Seconds Later
Pure unadulterated joy as the fans gathered in The Blob celebrate a fantastic victory… let the party begin!

10.30pm
The roars of victory turn to chants and songs and fans get ready for the presentation of the trophy…

10.30pm

Grown men hug each other, tears in their eyes. Friends text each other the news. Mile-wide smiles fill the room as the TV stations replay goals and incidents.

10.30pm

The following pictures really speak for themselves as supporters in The Blob just enjoy the moment their team become European Champions.

10.30pm
WALK ON…..

10.30pm
… WALK ON…

10.32pm
… WITH HOPE…

10.32pm
… IN YOUR HEART

10.33pm

....AND YOU'LL

10.34pm

... NEVER

10.34pm
… WALK ALONE …

10.34pm
YOU'LL NEVER WALK ALONE….

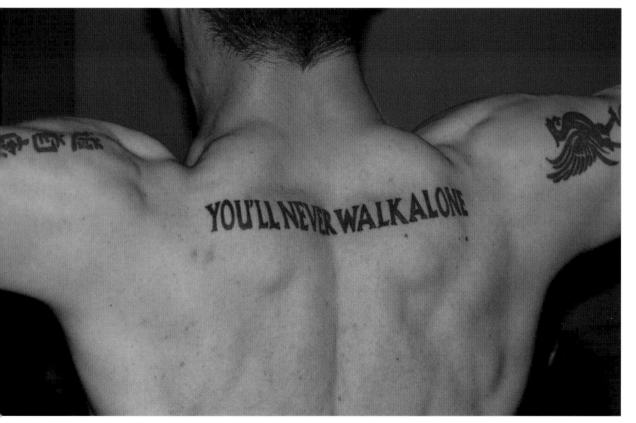

10.34pm
Still the noise rings in my ears and still the celebrations continue. Moments of sheer ecstasy!

10.36pm
The shirts have come off and now the champagne corks are popping. Standing opposite the bar, these lads give everyone a celebratory shower and the crowd lap it up!

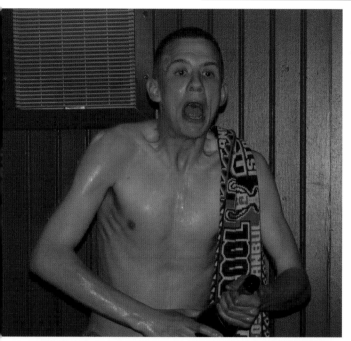

10.36pm

Wringing with sweat and champagne, he suddenly realises that some of the champers has found its way down the back of his Calvin Kleins!

10.37pm

He probably won't remember this, but he had his shirt almost off, his eyes were closed, he was standing on a table in the middle of a pub in Liverpool at twenty to eleven on a Wednesday night and for the fiftieth time that night he was singing "Oh When the reds go marching in"... and he'd never been happier!

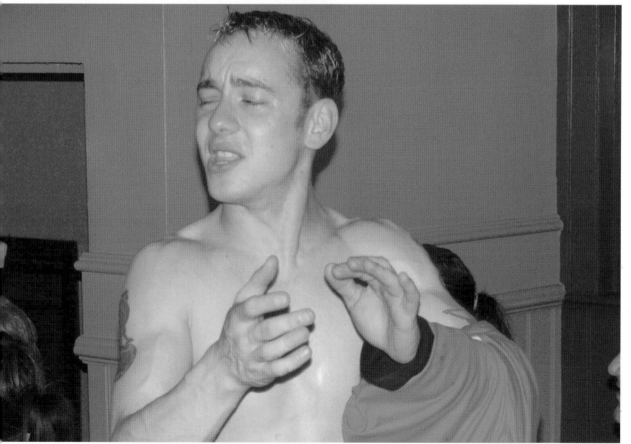

10.37pm

All some fans want to do is just stand and shout whilst others can't keep still. If you could bottle just one per cent of the sheer joy and elation here at the moment and sell it, you'd make millions!

10.37pm

Fans in champagne splattered shirts cheer their hearts out as once more the goals are re-played on the TV and the comeback and the penalties are relived.

10.38pm
With the clock at almost twenty to eleven, the lady on the phone can take no more as she's overcome by tears of joy.

10.39pm
The time to receive the trophy gets ever closer and before it's presented there's time for another rendition of "You'll never walk alone"... Sing your hearts out girls!

10.40pm
In the heat of celebration it doesn't matter that your scarf is upside down, because whichever way you look at it.. it's Liverpool v AC Milan and Liverpool are Champions! A serious pose that simply says "Job done"

10.42pm
Fans watch Stevie Gerrard walk to the podium to collect the Trophy. All eyes are on the screen and in a matter of a minute or so the city of Liverpool will erupt!

10.43pm
With seconds to go before it's lifted, fans watch Cisse, whose season was blighted with a serious injury, step forward and dance around the trophy.

10.45pm
Three hours after the first ball was kicked, Stevie Gerrard lifts the European Champions League trophy and in unison with bars all over the city, The Blob Shop goes wild!

10.45pm
The Champions of Europe are applauded

10.45pm
Mel is dancing on the chairs, the tears of earlier in the evening have long since dried as she's joining in the songs and chants with her fellow reds!

10.46pm

The party has well and truly begun! As the players parade the trophy in Istanbul, chants of "Are you watching Manchester?" bounce of the walls of the pub!

10.48pm

With hoards of other fans we tumble out into the city streets. All the time, the crowds are increasing and noise is getting louder. The name of Liverpool is chanted from all four corners of the city and car horns sound, adding to the atmosphere.

10.50pm

Another of those amazing co-incidences. Liverpool's first choice kit is red and their second choice is yellow… look! even the traffic lights are flashing in Liverpool colours and joining in the celebrations!

10.51pm

The guy on the right ran up to my daughter and kissed her…and then after I'd taken his picture with his mate, he turned his affection my way and kissed me!

10.52pm

Anything that can be climbed on, will be climbed on and this guy manages to scale a couple of telephone boxes.

10.52pm

Shirts off, waving them around in celebration. Has it sunk in yet I wonder?

10.53pm
"They'll never believe me when I tell them!"

10.55pm
Standing on railings, these guys don't look too steady, but what the hell, they support the European Champions… nothing else matters!

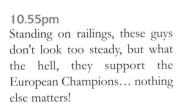

10.58pm
Back in Concert Square, the place is absolutely heaving. Cars try to make their way down the narrow streets but are surrounded by celebrating supporters.

10.58pm
Groups of fans stand on walls, cling to lampposts and try to hold on to each other as they sing in praise of the European Champions!

10.58pm
The noise from the square leaves a ringing in your ears, but, Istanbul apart, it's definitely the place to be... the following pictures capture the mood of the moment as the songs of Liverpool FC fill Concert Square

10.58pm
"Oh when the Reds, go marching in, I wanna be in that number... oh when the reds go marching in...."

10.58pm
"Steve Gerrard, Gerrard, he'll pass a ball 40 yards, he's big and he's f*****g hard…. Steve Gerrard, Gerrard"

10.59pm
"Rafa, Rafael, Rafa Rafael, Rafa Rafael, Rafael Benitez…

Rafa, Rafael, Rafa Rafael, Rafa Rafael, Rafael Benitez…"

10.59pm

"Are you watching?, Are you watching?, Are you watching Man-chest-er?"

10.59pm

"Walk on, walk on, with hope in your heart... and you'll never walk alone, you'll neeeeeeeever walk alone... walk on, walk on.... "

10.59pm
"L I V… E R P… double O L, LIVERPOOL FC!

L I V… E R P… double O L, LIVERPOOL FC"

11.00pm
"We all dream of a team of Carraghers… a team of Carraghers, a team of Carraghers… we all dream of a team of Carraghers…"

11.00pm
"All around the fields of Anfield Road, Where once we watched the King Kenny play (and could he play), We had Heighway on the wing, we had dreams and songs to sing… of the glory round the fields of Anfield Road"

11.03pm
Leaving Concert Square, we're heading back toward the centre once more. Thousands have now spilled onto the street. Vantage points are at a premium.

11.04pm
At first glance it looks like the guy with the shirt off is trying to scale the building, but in fact he was just trying to mount the horse!

11.04pm
These two guys should be in a circus with this kind of balancing act. Quite how people got to some of the places they managed to get to was a mystery!

11.04pm
The balancing act continues, though the guy on the left looks as though he could slide off any moment... he doesn't, well, he doesn't whilst I'm there, but no worries, there are police and paramedics on hand to deal with any minor accidents!

11.05pm
As the Radio City tower stands tall in the background, those at ground level know it was only a matter of time before the horse got mounted!

11.05pm

Some stand and point at people on statues, some are still singing, whilst one just stands and takes it all in…after all, moments like this are there to be treasured…

11.05pm

After you've won the European Champions League you're entitled to indulge in a little horse play…

11.06pm
Clinging on to a lamppost in the city centre, holding aloft the trophy and all around you is a sea of red… does it get any better than this?

11.06pm
More shirts are discarded; it's party time and there's dancing in the streets of the city!

11.08pm
An hour and twenty minutes since Gerrard lifted the trophy and the party is only just beginning!

11.08pm
Some fans have had to wait twenty years for a moment like this… for others it's come around a lot quicker… there's nothing like celebrating winning a trophy!

11.08pm
Time to leave Clayton Square and head for Williamson Square... one last look behind and still more people are spilling into the streets... air horns and car horns puncture the sound of fans cheering and singing

11.08pm
The banner reads... "In a town called Istanbul, there's a trophy to be won and we'll make it number 5 for LFC from Merseyside"

11.10pm

Walking through the streets and everyone has their own way of celebrating, some dance, some dance and sing, others just walk with their arms aloft savouring the moment!

11.10pm

If you're walking through a strange city at ten past eleven on a Wednesday evening and two lovely young ladies stop and ask you to take their picture, you have to oblige... well, you do, don't you?

11.10pm
As we head toward Williamson Square, we pass this guy flying the Liverpool flag.

11.11pm
Another reveller with a flag to fly, whilst to the right of the picture a couple indulge in "simultaneous texting"

11.16pm
Mel ventures under the water yet again, this time followed by a topless fan… male on this occasion!

11.16pm
With so many running through the water it was inevitable there would be collisions! As the two guys pick themselves up, one fan, in the background, puts himself forward for the wet-t-shirt competition!

11.16pm
An impromptu conga line breaks out in the fountain…with one guy not quite getting his bearings right!

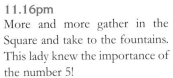

11.16pm
More and more gather in the Square and take to the fountains. This lady knew the importance of the number 5!

11.16pm
Through the arches of water and not a care in the world…Champions of Europe!

11.17pm
I looked at this guy and the way he was standing and thought... No! Surely he's not going to! I know he looks like he's about to… but thankfully I can assure you he didn't… !!!!

11.17pm
This guy takes a picture of himself whilst celebrating in the fountains. I couldn't help thinking he would wake up at some point the following day and wonder why his phone wasn't working…

11.17pm
"We're singing in the rain…just singing in the rain… what a glorious feeling, we've won it again!."

11.17pm
These ladies make a mad dash through the water, but still end up soaked!

11.18pm
You know you've won the European Champions League when you're stood in the middle of the city under a fountain, fully clothed and you don't give a damn!

11.18pm
"We've won the cup..

11.19pm
"We've won the cup… "

11.19pm
"Ee-Aye-Adio... we've won the cup"

11.19pm
The banner proclaims... "Rafa will win us a paella of trophies" Well, he's not made a bad start!

11.21pm
Friends re-united… these two chaps enjoy the fun-soaked celebrations that come with winning a European title. Everyone is still in party mood and the whole place is buzzing!

11.22pm
They danced through the fountain hand in hand….

11.23pm
They went through in pairs without their shirts on…

11.23pm
They went through alone, singing and waving flags….

11.25pm
Some fans are so excited by it all they are doing cartwheels…

11.25pm
There's only one way to describe the feeling……..
Just Champion!

11.25pm
"We are the Champions…"

11.26pm
"No time for losers, cos we are the Champions…. "

11.27pm
Shirt off, flag tucked in belt.. go for it…

11.27pm
Flag wavers run through the fountains with their flags trailing behind them… there's no letting up in the celebrations and everyone is still on a major high… and probably will be for weeks to come!

11.28pm
Time for a drink and where better to have it than under the water…

11.28pm
Yet another topless reveller but this one receives a cheer to rival that of Gerrard's first strike! Any ideas why?

11.29pm
The fountains are switched off and fans make the most of the last few drops of water.
As for Mel and I, we decide to head back to Albert Dock and the car

11.38pm
As we turn into Strand Street we pass a pub with a party in full swing. "The Leaving of Liverpool" is being sung loudly and through the open doors fans can be seen discussing the night's events. Mel wonders what it would be like at Anfield... so I tell her we'll find out!

...day 26th May
...0am

...ark up just round the
...r from Anfield and
...walk to the ground.
...in the city, the
...phere is something
.... cars drive by
...ing their horns, arms
...out of windows to
...the hands of fellow

...0am

...climb onto the gates
...field to celebrate and
...sore-throated
...ions of You'll never
...alone... In front of
...stadium stands the
...of Bill Shankly, and
...d his neck a
...pool scarf!

12:10am
Not for the first time this evening, the European Champions League trophy is held aloft and cheers ring out

12:10am
Fans conduct the choruses as in the streets below the fans again sing out the names of their heroes!

12:11am
Mel dances in the streets outside Anfield… weeks later and she's still dancing!

2am
akes a last look up at Anfield before we head back
e car and drive back to the Midlands. Twelve hours
ve set out and since then she's experienced every
ion possible.

r me, the dad, I just took pictures!

12:13am
Liverpool… Champions of Europe 2005!

 YOU'LL NEVER WALK ALONE
The End